Month/Year: ____________

MW00902461

Date	Item	QTY	Order #	Price			Notes
				Item	Shipping	Total	

Month/Year: ____________

Date	Item	QTY	Order #	Price			Notes
				Item	Shipping	Total	

Month/Year: ____________

Date	Item	QTY	Order #	Price			Notes
				Item	Shipping	Total	

Month/Year: ________________

Date	Item	QTY	Order #	Price			Notes
				Item	Shipping	Total	

Month/Year: ______________

Date	Item	QTY	Order #	Price			Notes
				Item	Shipping	Total	

Month/Year: ______________

Date	Item	QTY	Order #	Price			Notes
				Item	Shipping	Total	

Month/Year: ________________

Date	Item	QTY	Order #	Price			Notes
				Item	Shipping	Total	

Month/Year: ______________

Date	Item	QTY	Order #	Price			Notes
				Item	Shipping	Total	

Month/Year: ______________

Date	Item	QTY	Order #	Price			Notes
				Item	Shipping	Total	

Month/Year: ______________

Date	Item	QTY	Order #	Price			Notes
				Item	Shipping	Total	

Month/Year: ____________________

Date	Item	QTY	Order #	Price			Notes
				Item	Shipping	Total	

Month/Year: ____________

Date	Item	QTY	Order #	Price			Notes
				Item	Shipping	Total	

Month/Year: ______________

Date	Item	QTY	Order #	Price			Notes
				Item	Shipping	Total	

Month/Year: ______________

Date	Item	QTY	Order #	Price			Notes
				Item	Shipping	Total	

Month/Year: ____________

Date	Item	QTY	Order #	Price			Notes
				Item	Shipping	Total	

Month/Year: ____________

Date	Item	QTY	Order #	Price			Notes
				Item	Shipping	Total	

Month/Year: ____________________

Date	Item	QTY	Order #	Price			Notes
				Item	Shipping	Total	

Month/Year: ______________

Date	Item	QTY	Order #	Price			Notes
				Item	Shipping	Total	

Month/Year: ____________

Date	Item	QTY	Order #	Price			Notes
				Item	Shipping	Total	

Month/Year: ______________

Date	Item	QTY	Order #	Price			Notes
				Item	Shipping	Total	

Month/Year: ____________

Date	Item	QTY	Order #	Price			Notes
				Item	Shipping	Total	

Month/Year: ______________

Date	Item	QTY	Order #	Price			Notes
				Item	Shipping	Total	

Month/Year: ____________

Date	Item	QTY	Order #	Price			Notes
				Item	Shipping	Total	

Month/Year: ____________________

Date	Item	QTY	Order #	Price			Notes
				Item	Shipping	Total	

Month/Year: ______________

Date	Item	QTY	Order #	Price			Notes
				Item	Shipping	Total	

Month/Year: ______________

Date	Item	QTY	Order #	Price			Notes
				Item	Shipping	Total	

Month/Year: ____________________

Date	Item	QTY	Order #	Price			Notes
				Item	Shipping	Total	

Month/Year: ______________

Date	Item	QTY	Order #	Price			Notes
				Item	Shipping	Total	

Month/Year: ____________________

Date	Item	QTY	Order #	Price			Notes
				Item	Shipping	Total	

Month/Year: ____________

Date	Item	QTY	Order #	Price			Notes
				Item	Shipping	Total	

Month/Year: ______________

Date	Item	QTY	Order #	Price			Notes
				Item	Shipping	Total	

Month/Year: ____________________

Date	Item	QTY	Order #	Price			Notes
				Item	Shipping	Total	

Month/Year: ____________________

Date	Item	QTY	Order #	Price			Notes
				Item	Shipping	Total	

Month/Year: ______________

Date	Item	QTY	Order #	Price			Notes
				Item	Shipping	Total	

Month/Year: ________________

Date	Item	QTY	Order #	Price			Notes
				Item	Shipping	Total	

Month/Year: ________________

Date	Item	QTY	Order #	Price			Notes
				Item	Shipping	Total	

Month/Year: ____________________

Date	Item	QTY	Order #	Price			Notes
				Item	Shipping	Total	

Month/Year: ____________

Date	Item	QTY	Order #	Price			Notes
				Item	Shipping	Total	

Month/Year: ____________________

Date	Item	QTY	Order #	Price			Notes
				Item	Shipping	Total	

Month/Year: ________________

Date	Item	QTY	Order #	Price			Notes
				Item	Shipping	Total	

Month/Year: ____________________

Date	Item	QTY	Order #	Price			Notes
				Item	Shipping	Total	

Month/Year: ____________________

Date	Item	QTY	Order #	Price			Notes
				Item	Shipping	Total	

Month/Year: ________________

Date	Item	QTY	Order #	Price			Notes
				Item	Shipping	Total	

Month/Year: ______________

Date	Item	QTY	Order #	Price			Notes
				Item	Shipping	Total	

Month/Year: ____________________

Date	Item	QTY	Order #	Price			Notes
				Item	Shipping	Total	

Month/Year: ____________

Date	Item	QTY	Order #	Price			Notes
				Item	Shipping	Total	

Month/Year: ______________

Date	Item	QTY	Order #	Price			Notes
				Item	Shipping	Total	

Month/Year: ________________

Date	Item	QTY	Order #	Price			Notes
				Item	Shipping	Total	

Month/Year: ____________________

Date	Item	QTY	Order #	Price			Notes
				Item	Shipping	Total	

Month/Year: ______________

Date	Item	QTY	Order #	Price			Notes
				Item	Shipping	Total	

Month/Year: ____________________

Date	Item	QTY	Order #	Price			Notes
				Item	Shipping	Total	

Month/Year: ____________

Date	Item	QTY	Order #	Price			Notes
				Item	Shipping	Total	

Month/Year: ____________________

Date	Item	QTY	Order #	Price			Notes
				Item	Shipping	Total	

Month/Year: ____________________

Date	Item	QTY	Order #	Price			Notes
				Item	Shipping	Total	

Month/Year: ____________

Date	Item	QTY	Order #	Price			Notes
				Item	Shipping	Total	

Month/Year: ______________

Date	Item	QTY	Order #	Price			Notes
				Item	Shipping	Total	

Month/Year: ____________

Date	Item	QTY	Order #	Price			Notes
				Item	Shipping	Total	

Month/Year: ______________

Date	Item	QTY	Order #	Price			Notes
				Item	Shipping	Total	

Month/Year: ____________________

Date	Item	QTY	Order #	Price			Notes
				Item	Shipping	Total	

Month/Year: ______________

Date	Item	QTY	Order #	Price			Notes
				Item	Shipping	Total	

Month/Year: ________________

Date	Item	QTY	Order #	Price			Notes
				Item	Shipping	Total	

Month/Year: ________________

Date	Item	QTY	Order #	Price			Notes
				Item	Shipping	Total	

Month/Year: ______________

Date	Item	QTY	Order #	Price			Notes
				Item	Shipping	Total	

Month/Year: ________________

Date	Item	QTY	Order #	Price			Notes
				Item	Shipping	Total	

Month/Year: ____________________

Date	Item	QTY	Order #	Price			Notes
				Item	Shipping	Total	

Month/Year: ______________

Date	Item	QTY	Order #	Price			Notes
				Item	Shipping	Total	

Month/Year: ____________________

Date	Item	QTY	Order #	Price			Notes
				Item	Shipping	Total	

Month/Year: ______________

Date	Item	QTY	Order #	Price			Notes
				Item	Shipping	Total	

Month/Year: ________________

Date	Item	QTY	Order #	Price			Notes
				Item	Shipping	Total	

Month/Year: ____________

Date	Item	QTY	Order #	Price			Notes
				Item	Shipping	Total	

Month/Year: ____________________

Date	Item	QTY	Order #	Price			Notes
				Item	Shipping	Total	

Month/Year: ______________

Date	Item	QTY	Order #	Price			Notes
				Item	Shipping	Total	

Month/Year: ____________

Date	Item	QTY	Order #	Price			Notes
				Item	Shipping	Total	

Month/Year: ______________

Date	Item	QTY	Order #	Price			Notes
				Item	Shipping	Total	

Month/Year: ____________

Date	Item	QTY	Order #	Price			Notes
				Item	Shipping	Total	

Month/Year: ____________

Date	Item	QTY	Order #	Price			Notes
				Item	Shipping	Total	

Month/Year: ____________________

Date	Item	QTY	Order #	Price			Notes
				Item	Shipping	Total	

Month/Year: ______________

Date	Item	QTY	Order #	Price			Notes
				Item	Shipping	Total	

Month/Year: ______________

Date	Item	QTY	Order #	Price			Notes
				Item	Shipping	Total	

Month/Year: ______________

Date	Item	QTY	Order #	Price			Notes
				Item	Shipping	Total	

Month/Year: ______________

Date	Item	QTY	Order #	Price			Notes
				Item	Shipping	Total	

Month/Year: ________________

Date	Item	QTY	Order #	Price			Notes
				Item	Shipping	Total	

Month/Year: ____________________

Date	Item	QTY	Order #	Price			Notes
				Item	Shipping	Total	

Month/Year: ____________

Date	Item	QTY	Order #	Price			Notes
				Item	Shipping	Total	

Month/Year: ____________________

Date	Item	QTY	Order #	Price			Notes
				Item	Shipping	Total	

Month/Year: ______________

Date	Item	QTY	Order #	Price			Notes
				Item	Shipping	Total	

Month/Year: ____________

Date	Item	QTY	Order #	Price			Notes
				Item	Shipping	Total	

Month/Year: ____________

Date	Item	QTY	Order #	Price			Notes
				Item	Shipping	Total	

Month/Year: ____________

Date	Item	QTY	Order #	Price			Notes
				Item	Shipping	Total	

Month/Year: ____________

Date	Item	QTY	Order #	Price			Notes
				Item	Shipping	Total	

Month/Year: ____________________

Date	Item	QTY	Order #	Price			Notes
				Item	Shipping	Total	

Month/Year: ____________________

Date	Item	QTY	Order #	Price			Notes
				Item	Shipping	Total	

Month/Year: ______________

Date	Item	QTY	Order #	Price			Notes
				Item	Shipping	Total	

Month/Year: ______________

Date	Item	QTY	Order #	Price			Notes
				Item	Shipping	Total	

Month/Year: ______________

Date	Item	QTY	Order #	Price			Notes
				Item	Shipping	Total	

Month/Year: ______________

Date	Item	QTY	Order #	Price			Notes
				Item	Shipping	Total	

Month/Year: ______________

Date	Item	QTY	Order #	Price			Notes
				Item	Shipping	Total	

Month/Year: ____________

Date	Item	QTY	Order #	Price			Notes
				Item	Shipping	Total	

Month/Year: ____________________

Date	Item	QTY	Order #	Price			Notes
				Item	Shipping	Total	

Month/Year: ______________

Date	Item	QTY	Order #	Price			Notes
				Item	Shipping	Total	

Made in the USA
Las Vegas, NV
04 April 2024

88237013R00063